AF451561

WHAT HAPPENED TO MY BOUNTY?

WHAT HAPPENED TO MY BOUNTY?

An inspiring story about the art of risk management according to ISO 31000

Peter Blokland

Author: Peter Blokland, PhD
Cover design: Peter Blokland & Freepik
ISBN: 9789403786896
© 2025 BYAZ bv & Peter Blokland
Telephone: +32 (0) 34584803
E-mail: peter.blokland@byaz.be
Publisher:
Storyland, Nijverheidsstraat 70, 2160 Wommelgem, België

NOTICE TO THE READER

For

Liam, Maya, Maxim, Liz & Emilie

and an excellent future for all of us

Acknowledgments

I extend my heartfelt gratitude to everyone who has contributed to the creation of this booklet through their conversations, feedback, and insights. Your input has been invaluable throughout this journey.

A special thanks goes to my wife and family, whose unwavering support, motivation, and inspiration continue to fuel my writing. Without their presence, this work would not have been possible.

Finally, I wish to express my sincere appreciation to Prof. Dr. Ir. Genserik Reniers, my steadfast companion in exploring the deeper meaning of risk, safety, and performance. Together, we have delved into how these concepts can be approached in meaningful and impactful ways. This booklet is, in many ways, a reflection of those shared endeavours.

Table of contents

Author's Note   3

Foreword   5

A special networking event   7

The Valley and the Main Characters   9

Settlements in the Valley   23

Unexpected Events   31

A Smart Move   41

Another Challenge for the Valley   45

Epilogue   53

Appendix   57

Author's Note

"*What happened to my bounty?*" explores the risks that arise in life, represented through the metaphor of a "bounty," symbolizing the objectives (results to be achieved) one strives for. Whether personal, organizational, or societal. Inspired by "*Who Moved My Cheese?*" by Dr Spencer Johnson, I sought to write a similarly accessible story about risk and risk management, highlighting their importance and challenges.

My academic journey, culminating in a PhD at TU Delft in 2023, deepened my understanding of risk, safety, and performance, three interconnected concepts centred on objectives (results to be achieved). Risk pertains to objectives in the future, safety focuses on the present, and performance reflects outcomes after objectives have been managed (or not). I concluded that managing based on results or safety is reactive, while risk management is inherently proactive, enabling decisions that shape a more certain future.

In our VUCA (volatile, uncertain, complex, ambiguous) world, routine actions have become unreliable, and constant change has increased uncertainty. The interconnected nature of society and the overload of ambiguous information make decision-making more complex. Additionally, the pressures of societal and personal ambitions in a fragile, fear-driven BANI (brittle, anxious, non-linear, incomprehensible) world create stress at all levels, individual, organizational, and societal.

This booklet aims to simplify risk management and demonstrate its critical importance in addressing today's challenges. Effective risk management is essential for creating and sustaining value, enabling managers to combine sustainability, performance, and safety. It offers a framework for making informed decisions and achieving goals with greater certainty in an ever-changing environment.

Lastly, the characters in this story are inspired by concepts and terms from the world of risk management, their names reflecting key ideas or characteristics. Can you uncover them all?

Peter Blokland, PhD

Foreword

In this new book, Peter, a born storyteller, takes the reader in tow in a modern risk fairy tale. Based on metaphors and analogies, important messages are entrusted regarding risks and the ins and outs of companies. Readers' interpretations may differ, and the "health lessons" learned from them may apply to each specific organization. Peter's goal is undoubtedly to get people to reflect on risks and to teach them to 'think about risks', in order to make better and more thoughtful decisions in their work context, but also in their own lives.

This booklet gives rise to asking questions and looking for answers. The basis of adequate risk thinking starts with asking questions, continues with a critical view of the environment and ends with a 'situational awareness' attitude. That threefold goal is exactly what I think this book can achieve. I wish the reader a lot of fun reading it and good luck in implementing it.

Prof. Dr. Ir. Genserik Reniers

A special networking event

On a pleasant summer evening, Geraint Kammens mingled with a colourful group of entrepreneurs, visionaries and specialists at a vibrant conference. The room exuded ambition and cooperation, while ideas and stories rolled through the space like waves. It was a place where every encounter offered opportunities, and every thought unleashed inspiration.

Amid this energetic exchange, Geraint met Vivianne Ventura, a seasoned entrepreneur, who spoke about the need for resilience in an unpredictable market. "Every decision seems like a gamble," she sighed. A little further on, he heard Danny Advité, a high-tech visionary, talking passionately about the speed of technological change and the challenge of keeping up with innovation. "Complexity is growing faster than ever," he emphasized.

He also came across Naomi Constrad, a strategist with foresight. She said that companies must respond flexibly to the whims of the customer. "The old models don't work anymore," she said firmly. Financial expert Roger Marfinex, meanwhile, argued for robust risk management, pointing to the fragility of financial systems: "We have to be prepared for unexpected shocks."

These powerful stories of adaptation, innovation and resilience resonated as a symphony of shared challenges in today's dynamic and complex world. Geraint sensed that the undercurrent of uncertainty touched many. In the meantime, he gathered valuable insights from experienced leaders such as Sandra Doldts. She was an expert of strategic planning.

Everyone contributed to a collective understanding: only with vision and agility can one embrace an uncertain future.

In the middle of the lively crowd, a serene silence fell as Iris Tetynohko stepped forward. Her warm smile and confident appearance filled the room, and the attendees, entrepreneurs, visionaries and leaders, listened intently to her every word. Iris, the driving force behind this special gathering, welcomed them with a voice that radiated both authority and warmth.

"It's great to see you all here," she began. "As we strengthen old ties and forge new connections, I want to share a story with you. It has changed my perspective on business. It gave me a different perspective on our daily search for better results and success."

The audience held its breath when Iris started to talk. It was a compelling parable about a valley, with special characters and unexpected challenges. She painted a story that went beyond just the words. It was a lesson, a mirror for the choices and ambitions of her audience. As she spoke, even the most seasoned experts became captivated. Sandra Doldts and Mr. Esoco exchanged glances, the story raised questions about their own assumptions and strategies.

The circle around Iris grew rapidly. Everyone was carried away by her words. Geraint Kammens also felt how her story completely took hold of him.

"This," Iris said with a meaningful pause, "is how the story goes..."

The Valley and the Main Characters

In the distant echoes of forgotten times, in a land veiled by the mists of history, a remarkable community flourished nestled in a mysterious valley. This valley was an area of untapped potential, hidden dangers, and formidable trials. But what really set this community apart was the way they approached life in the valley and how they dealt with the multifaceted challenges they faced. For the observant viewer, the divergences between the different characters became apparent remarkably quickly.

Every day, the inhabitants of the valley embarked on a relentless search for results, pursuing their "bounty" with unwavering devotion. The bounty was the fruit of their labour, and the taste of success was often sweeter than the ripest fruits you could pick in the valley. What distinguished these remarkable individuals from one another was the diversity in their approach to their pursuit of their bounty.

The setting sun, which looked out over the intriguing image of the vast valley like a silent witness, covered it with golden hues and sprinkled the whole with fascinating shadows. It quickly became clear that the valley, like an ever-changing maze, presented both threats and opportunities. The bounty, which symbolized the compensation for the achievements of the valley's inhabitants, was attractive but often elusive. To pursue this needed a lot of adaptability and courage from these inhabitants of the valley. The invisible challenges were like the fleeting shadows that lurked beneath the surface of apparent prosperity. They reflected the unforeseen events that could cause even the best-laid plans to fail.

"Everyone strives for a bounty,

But each does this in his own way."

In the face of the need to embrace change, one quickly saw the universal truth that the landscape of life is constantly changing and sometimes this happened very quickly. Those who navigated through it with resilience and an open mind were therefore often better armed to thrive in it. The valley, with its twists and turns, was like a blank slate, ready to receive the report of the struggle with which the people tried to resist the force of change, or on the other hand to write down the story of how they managed to embrace these events with an inquisitive mind, hungry for improvement, growth and sustainability.

In the murmur of voices and laughter down in the valley one could clearly hear what was going on. The wonderful stories of triumphs and trials were eagerly shared with each other. And the testimonies of resilience and adaptability, necessary for the adventures that unfolded in the valley, went smoothly from mouth to mouth. However, the inhabitants of the valley did not realize that they were not just a collection of characters, they were part of a microcosm, populated with ever-evolving opportunities and challenges. The paths were winding, and the mind-set of discovery and growth was a constant given.

When you travelled through the valley, you soon came across a clearly distinguishable character. This valley dweller seemed to be completely absorbed in the "now" and reacted impulsively to every circumstance that crossed her path. There was little sign of deep contemplation or strategic foresight in her approach to her journey through the valley. Her name was Serena Dipity, and her motto was like "Carpe diem". She lived each day as it unfolded before her. She embraced the events of the moment without too many worries or thinking about things.

"A bounty does not come on its own.

It is the fruit of effort and the pursuit of objectives."

Soon you realized that Serena's adventures in the valley were a continuous dance of lively spontaneity. It was like a melody of joyful wanderlust that resounded in every step she took. In this enigmatic realm of unknown opportunities and hidden dangers, Serena was the embodiment of the incorrigible optimist.

With a heart that wasn't weighed down by the weight of her past missteps or worries about future uncertainties, Serena lived in the present. She was a beacon of enthusiasm and hope for those who crossed her path. After all, her wanderings were guided by an unshakable faith in the grand design of the universe. She followed the paths that winded through the valley as fate bestowed upon her, her eyes fixed on the horizon of a happy future.

Serena knew no fear of the unexplored territory. In her pursuit of abundance, she danced with the mysteries of life and embraced the idea that the valley held untold wonders waiting for her to be discovered. Like a fresh breeze, she went with the flow through the meadows of the valley, letting the unexpected unfold before her at its own pace.

She didn't wonder what was in store for her; Instead, she enjoyed every moment and reaped the benefits of her journey with a smile on her face. After all, Serena's bounty was not only the tangible treasures she collected, but it was also the elusive moments of joy and wonder that enriched her soul as she wandered through the valley.

Looking at Serena's approach to pursuing her bounty, one could see that it is a testimony to the beauty of living in the moment, embracing uncertainty as a canvas for life's surprises, where cherishing the journey is just as important as reaching the destination itself.

"What risks would you dare to take if you weren't
afraid of the risks run?"

Exploring the valley further, among the countless possibilities and lurking dangers, another figure came into view. This person was known as Dodger Dagner. He embodied an approach to the uncertainties in the valley that contrasted sharply with the actions of Serena Dipity. Dodger was completely attuned to the dangers of the valley. On his way to bounty, he traversed the terrain of the valley as a cautious traveller, constantly vigilant and wary of the shadows cast by uncertainty. Dodger was very steadfast in his efforts to assess the degree of uncertainty related to those hazards and their potential impact on the bounty. He therefore kept extensive reports about it, which he handed over to his boss, if necessary, in the hope that he would do the right things with it to achieve their bounty.

Dodger's search for his bounty was closely intertwined with someone else, it came through Mr. Endever and his wishes. Dodger worked for Mr. Endever, whose entrepreneurial spirit often clashed with Dodger's risk-averse nature. Dodger, who rarely ventured into uncharted territory, was drawn to the sure, ingrained, and familiar routes that gave him a sense of security. The certainty of the known was his refuge, and he clung to it with a tenacity that grew out of his striving to avoid especially the invisible dangers that might creep in the valley.

Dodger often advised Mr. Endever not to take any risks, knowing that his sometimes-adventurous intentions could lead to trouble. Because for Dodger Dagner, every trip through the valley was a meticulous expedition. With the eye of an expert, he consulted the testimonies of his past experiences, keenly aware of the characteristics of misfortune and missteps. He knew that the terrain held both opportunities and dangers, and he was determined to avoid the latter. However, Mr. Endever was always looking for new ways to increase their bounty.

"The more important the bounty is to you, the more risks you're willing to take and run to achieve it."

That's why he saw Dodger more than once as a fun spoiler who spoiled the fun of his adventures in the valley.

Endever's approach to pursuing bounty, in turn, was characterized by seizing opportunities when the opportunity arose. But also, by changing his mind when it suited him. Methodical planning and an unwavering commitment to avoiding the unknown and dangers were not really his thing. While Dodger Dagner meticulously charted his course through the valley, marking every known obstacle and danger and making sure he was well prepared for any threat that might come his way, Mr. Endever often ignored the warnings Dodger gave. Endever's journey through the valley was at times deliberate and calculated but rarely guided by a deep-seated need to protect them from the uncertainties and dangers of the valley or to tread the chosen path with caution.

Deeper in the valley, one would soon come across Faith Destiny. Her approach to the valley was a testimony to her exceptional instincts and her unwavering faith in her intuition. This was characterized by her steadfast confidence and her willingness to embrace risks when they felt right to her. Faith

possessed a unique ability to sense the subtle shifts in the landscape and to perceive opportunities and threats with remarkable precision. She didn't shy away from challenges, but instead actively sought out opportunities when she understood the intricacies of a situation. Her journey through the valley was guided by a deep connection with her inner compass and she distinguished herself by her decisiveness. It often led to successful actions, as she fearlessly grabbed her bounty when the path was clear.

However, Faith Destiny was no stranger to the treacherous nature of the valley. She understood that life, like any landscape, could be full of uncertainties and potential dangers.

"Keep your bounty in sight enough to know when it
no longer brings a smile on your face."

When her keen instincts warned her of unclear situations or impending dangers, she did not rush headlong into the unknown. Instead, she would exercise caution and restraint, knowing that not all bounties were worth pursuing. Faith refrained from action when the situation was too unclear or posed unnecessary risks, choosing wisdom over recklessness. Her approach to the valley intuitively combined boldness and caution, making her an inspiring and versatile character on life's journey.

Deep in the valley, one would eventually find brother and sister Gains and Troubles Lifferalitoye and soon discover that they are intriguing figures. They were twins and looked like the two sides of the same coin. Each had a unique approach to both finding and keeping their bounty. Their collaborative approach to ensuring they could capture and secure the value of their bounty was truly remarkable.

Gains, with his eternal optimism and boundless enthusiasm, saw the valley as an infinite pool of possibilities. He was the dreamer, the visionary who was constantly scanning the horizon for untapped potential. For him, there were no limits to what could be achieved in the valley. Gains was not only a dreamer, but also an innovation architect. He spun together grand visions that stretched far beyond the horizon of the valley, devised new strategies for prosperity and shaped their future.

His adventurous spirit thrived in exploring the unknown and unexplored territory further down the valley and he encouraged others to join in joint exploration. Gains believed in the power of teamwork and wider collaboration and saw this as the key to unlocking the valley's untapped potential.

However, Troubles, Gains' sister, played a crucial role in their journey. She recognized the importance of balance and a well-

"An open mind helps in discovering (new) bounties."

prepared approach, in which clear agreements can best be made in advance. While admiring her brother's boundless creativity and potential to create a future, Troubles was the voice of reason. She looked at Gains' plans in an organized and dutiful way for possible imperfections and vulnerabilities. When she identified these, she gave constructive criticism and then showed the possible pitfalls that needed to be addressed first to best secure the new paths to bounty.

For Troubles, the valley was a place of both opportunity and caution. She believed in the importance of aligning dreams with everyday reality. Her role was not to stifle Gain's creativity, but to further refine it and ensure that their joint journey to bounty was purposeful and resilient. Troubles knew that her partnership with Gains was of a strategic nature, with each playing a crucial role. Gains dreamed, and she refined it into a high-performance and safe plan. And so, together, they created a dynamic that was essential to harnessing the valley's true potential. Together, Gains and Troubles were a harmonious blend of creativity and soundness, making their journey through the valley harmonious and prosperous.

"The better you manage risks, the sooner you'll
find and get bounties."

Settlements in the Valley

Over time, one would get a better view of the valley and its inhabitants. There are also the various locations where these figures stayed.

At the settlement where Serena Dipity resided, one could see a special form of nonchalance that you would not find anywhere else. As you might have guessed, Serena went into the valley with an uninhibited spirit, determined to find her bounty. She followed the natural paths and collected what she encountered on her way and what appealed to her. Of course, she made the occasional misstep and got into trouble for wrong decisions, but gradually she learned to recognize the pitfalls and slippery spots of the valley. Serena discovered through experience what was useful and edible and continued her joyful journey with determination, ready to reap the bounties of her efforts.

Soon she gathered a number of followers around her and so a settlement arose around the place where Serena was staying. It was a place that fully reflected her character. In this settlement there was a feeling of freedom and happiness that translated into a rather chaotic spectacle. Paths randomly meandered through the settlement, with no clear structure or plan. Dwellings may have seemed charming at first glance, but upon closer inspection, you could see that they were built randomly, without regard to the place where they were erected, or they testified to a lack of attention to the materials that made them up.

The residents behaved like free spirits, without clear rules or guidelines. There was no fixed plan to be discovered in their daily activities. Apparently, they were confident that coincidences and daily impulses would yield a bounty. This lack of structured approach was also reflected in the way they moved around the settlement, seemingly without a clear and bright goal in mind.

Foresight was apparently a foreign concept for this group. The residents seemed completely unaware of the various possibilities that could arise. After all, their houses had been built without regard for the unpredictability of the weather, and their choices in the valley were more like following where the wind blows than conducting sophisticated and efficient planning.

In short, the settlement of Serena Dipity was like a picturesque scene that, on closer inspection, revealed the absence of any efficiency and planning. It was a place where spontaneity reigned supreme, but where the price of this unbridled freedom could rise high if the storms of uncertainty hit.

Further down the valley, deeper into the hidden, you came across Dodger Dagner's village. This was controlled by the rather ruthless leader, Mr. Endever. Dodger's approach to traversing and discovering the valley contrasted rather strongly with Mr. Endever's focus on quick success and making gains with as little effort as possible. The village reflected this sometimes-contradictory mentality in every aspect of its existence.

At Dodger Dagner's home one could find a completely different situation than what could be seen earlier in Serena's place. The quarter where he lived accurately reflected his mentality. The streets were laid out in a well-arranged manner and the houses testified to a well-thought-out and traditional construction, based on well-known building plans. A clear, organized and structured approach could be seen everywhere. In other places in the village you could find other things, ranging from gaudy houses to sometimes ragged huts, depending on how well the residents knew Mr. Endever and whether they were in good standing with him.

Dodger watched the actions of the villagers in the valley with great caution. If necessary, he would visit the unknown paths thoughtfully and inquisitively, always looking for possible dangers. He remained true to the insights of previous experiences and preferred to skip many, previously unknown, possibilities. His progress was steady, but he avoided pitfall trails and made sure he didn't encounter too many slippery spots. For Dodger, the motto was: rather let an opportunity pass than look for unnecessary obstacles.

Meanwhile, Mr. Endever's journey through the valley was marked by his focus on quick wins and gains without putting in too much effort. He was drawn to strategies that immediately held out the prospect of bounty, often consciously overlooking the long-term implications and hazards for the village and valley. While Dodger prioritized caution and sticking to familiar routes, Endever pursued shortcuts and easy wins, which often led to disagreements and friction with among the villagers.

This contrast in approaches also created tension in the village, as Dodger's cautious demeanour clashed with Mr. Endever's pursuit of quick results. While Dodger advocated stability and predictability, Mr. Endever prioritized immediate gains, sometimes at the expense of longer-term sustainability.

The villagers valued control, conservatism, and often showed resistance to change, reflecting Dodger's preference for caution and stability. This was in contrast to the focus of Endever who preferred quick success and immediate bounties. This attitude of regularly seeking immediate and seemingly obvious bounty often led to conflicts with Dodger Dagner and the other residents of the village.

Traveling further through the valley, one would discover another distinct situation at Faith Destiny. Faith was a master at intuitively choosing the right routes and quickly achieved the fruits that the valley had to offer. Her intuition led her directly to promising places, and she was often the first to discover and exploit them before others did. Once she had exploited the potential of a location, she intuitively moved on, looking for new possibilities. Soon a group of residents arose, who dealt with the valley in their own way.

In the entrepreneurial enclave of Faith Destiny, the dynamic was as unpredictable as her personal approach. The streets meandered through the village, reflecting how residents intuitively discovered new routes to achieve their goals.

The architecture of the houses showed a certain eccentricity, adapted to the unique vision of each resident. Creative additions and expansions reflected the unpredictable uniqueness of intuitive entrepreneurship. The village exuded an atmosphere of constant change, where old structures constantly gave way to new, intuitively led initiatives.

The inhabitants embraced new ideas with full enthusiasm and quickly adapted to these opportunities, which meant that the village was constantly evolving. Constant movement and adaptation were the characteristics. Business was quickly left behind as residents intuitively moved on to new opportunities.

Decision-making did not follow a traditional, methodical path. Often it was seemingly impulsive and moment-bound, aimed at seizing new opportunities. The village was therefore an exciting, vibrant and innovative place, where new ideas were constantly flourishing. Sometimes there were insufficient opportunities for these ideas to come to fruition and the lack of structure and common concepts made it difficult for this enclave to grow.

Finally, in the deepest part of the valley, one would reach the region of Gains and Troubles who worked meticulously together to pick out the most promising paths. They explored the terrain thoroughly, looking for opportunities and dangers. Gains was tireless in his search for new opportunities, while Troubles watched over the potential pitfalls and slippery spots that a new path brought. Together, they made sure that Gains did not recklessly walk unknown paths, but first carefully researched the circumstances. If there were obstacles, they worked together to overcome them. Cushioning pitfalls and tackling slippery spots allowed them to move forward safely and reap the hidden benefits concealed behind these obstacles. In this way, they could walk the paths that others avoided again and again, without being in danger, while taking advantage of the great bounty that the valley had to offer them.

Gains and Troubles worked side by side, sharing their insights and vision with the people around them. This was reflected in the architecture of the village, giving it a perfect balance of innovation and stability.

In the area where Gains and Troubles worked together, there were few residents at first, but soon a harmonious scene unfolded. Streets were thoughtfully laid out, with a clearly structured layout that reflected the thorough exploration of the site. These streets were not only linear, but rather winding, with an opportunity to seize behind every bend and a potential risk of going after each side path. The twists and turns were functional and provided an attractive living environment.

The houses in this settlement were an example of integral design. They were adapted to the vision of the residents, where creativity and functionality went hand in hand. Nevertheless, they were built based on common concepts and a shared, overarching vision for this place of residence so that people did not get in each other's way and the communal facilities could be used efficiently.

They became adept at quickly adapting the residents to new ideas and opportunities. There was a constant sense of movement and adaptation, abandoning old or worn-out things in favour of new, well-thought-out initiatives. It was a vibrant and functional community where Gains and Troubles based their decision-making on a thoroughly constructed and clear process that could be applied quickly when needed, but also accommodate extensive studies when projects necessitated it.

After all, the decision-making in this village did not follow a rigid path but was rather an iterative process with the necessary flexibility. Gains brought ideas and opportunities, while Troubles carefully assessed the potential threats. Together, they thought about possible routes and methods, discussed obstacles, anticipated pitfalls, and made the paths safe to walk. It was a place where integrated action reigned and where this was not just a process but became a way of life.

And so, it seemed in the atmospheric and vibrant landscape of the valley that everyone, each with their own unique approach, experienced an era of abundance.

Serena, the adventurous dancer of life, had found joy in every flower she picked, every song she hummed, and enjoyed the warmth of the sun on her skin. The valley offered her abundant joy and cheerfulness.

Mr. Endever's pursuit of quick wins and bounty without putting in much effort often led to conflicts with Dodger and others in the village but brought enough bounty to continue this approach. While Dodger prioritized long-term stability and durability, Mr. Endever's focus on immediate return on investment often clashed with Dodger's cautious approach. These conflicts highlighted the tension between Dodger's preference for caution and stability and Mr. Endever's relentless pursuit of short-term gain, sharpening the divergent paths of the village's leaders.

Faith Destiny, the intuitive sage, led her troops through the valley with confidence. She knew when to act and when to wait, when to take risks and when to exercise restraint. Her bounty came from a balance between daring and insight.

Gains and Troubles Lifferalitoye, the dynamic duo, was the epitome of collaboration. Their efforts led to boundless creativity and careful planning, turning every challenge into an opportunity to be exploited. They reaped the benefits of teamwork and strategy, allowing their settlement to grow and prosper at a constant rate.

It was a time of abundance in the valley, where the harvests were plentiful, the worries melted like snow in the sun and where the inhabitants walked the paths of the valley happily and carefree. But as is often the case in life: all great songs do not last forever.

"If risks are not (properly) managed, things can
go wrong very quickly and drastically."

Unexpected Events

Suddenly, an unexpected and threatening scene unfolded in the idyllic valley. The harmonious and cheerful rhythm of society was rudely disrupted by the arrival of a pack of hungry wolves. The residents, accustomed to a comfortable existence, were suddenly confronted with a terrifying reality. Their quiet life turned into a struggle for survival, with the once-safe valley becoming a place of danger and uncertainty.

Serena, the good-humoured inspirer of her settlement, faced an unprecedented challenge. The wolves put her optimistic approach to life to the test. Instead of being prepared for this potential threat, the settlement had allowed itself to be lulled by a false sense of security. Now, Serena, with her positive attitude, had to motivate and lead the community through this unexpected crisis.

But the hungry wolves roamed the streets in search of prey. The previously quiet and peaceful settlement was now steeped in fear and chaos. Houses that had once been built with a lack of foresight now proved vulnerable to the threat from outside. The residents, accustomed to a cheerful existence, did not know how to react. The lack of preparation and the inability to act adequately made them easy prey for the wolves.

Serena, who had always been used to going with the flow of the moment, was now confronted with a harsh truth. The lack of foresight meant that there was no organized response to this unexpected threat. The settlement, which thrived on impulsive decisions, now discovered that a lack of preparation could have disastrous consequences.

The wolves plundered and destroyed what they met, including the bounty that had been built up in the settlement. The wolves devoted significant attention to it and without a solid basis to fall back on, the residents saw the bounty slip away irretrievably through their hands. The chaos that followed illustrated the usefulness and necessity of greater foresight in a world that inevitably produced such unforeseen challenges. The settlement of Serena, once a symbol of lack of prudence, learned the hard way that a lack of anticipation of unexpected events could be a costly mistake.

The settlement fell apart completely, and Serena was faced with a choice: leave the valley immediately or look for a new place for her activities. Instead of fleeing headlong into an uncertain future, she understood that cooperation offered her best chance of survival. She turned to Gains and Troubles, knowing that they were known for their willingness to cooperate and their shared commitment to the well-being of the entire valley. Together, as a united front, they could potentially brave the hungry wolves and protect the valley.

Dodger Dagner had somehow foreseen the arrival of wolves and other threats, a testament to his cautious nature and unwavering vigilance. He took prompt action and advised Mr. Endever on possible measures to combat this threat. Strengthening the village walls could guarantee the safety of the inhabitants and stockpiling supplies for the people of the village would ensure a better chance of survival in case calamities would ravage them. It was wise counsel that could be invaluable. However, Dodger also realized that even within the safe confines of this sanctuary, stark restrictions could loom. Because although Dodger advised anticipating the possibility of a long-term crisis, he was also confronted with the harrowing choices that would have to be made in such a case in function of the attention and budgets that Mr. Endever would want to spend on a village wall and supplies. He was particularly concerned about those who might fall outside the village walls, both animals and people. He struggled with the weight of his advice, aware of the moral dilemmas and far-reaching consequences it entailed. Realizing that his council would inform Mr. Endever's decisions, Dodger felt the immense burden of responsibility weigh heavily upon him.

With an unwavering belief in the paramount importance of caution for survival, Dodger offered his suggestions to Mr. Endever, advocating for measures that prioritized collective efforts and long-term sustainability. As the final decision-maker, however, Mr. Endever had the authority to determine the course of the village. Dodger could only watch, hopeful but apprehensive, as Mr. Endever weighed the options for him.

Mr. Endever chose the path of least effort and decided to build the wall in such a way that it would only allow the animals and people who could contribute to immediate profit and quick success even in crisis. He preferred short-term benefits to long-term stability. Although Dodger's advice emphasized the tension between the distinct options and emphasized the divergent path chosen by the village's leader, Endever maintained the decision to pursue the short-term outcomes.

Despite Dodger's wise advice, Mr. Endever's decisions ultimately determined the fate of the village when the wolves raided the valley. It led to conflicts and moral dilemmas that also tested Dodger's resolve. As the wolves mercilessly preyed on the vulnerable creatures that were exposed, Dodger watched from the safety of his enclosure, grappling with the consequences of the decisions made by another's hand. Amid the conflict between caution and expediency, Dodger remained steadfast in its commitment to stability, even as Mr. Endever

"It is safer to go elsewhere than to stay in a place with no bounty."

pursued quick and easy results. But there was no bounty for the villagers who stayed behind.

Faith Destiny, adept at sensing opportunities even before they reveal themselves, discovered the imminent danger of the wolves. Her gut feeling forced her to act at once. She quickly left the enclave and, with only a few people who decided to follow her, strategically retreated to a safer position in the valley, a place where she could find both the protection she was looking for and space to continue working towards her ambitious goals. It wasn't an easy choice, as she realized that she had to put aside some of the promising opportunities she'd already set in motion until the situation was safer. However, the threat of the wolves was undeniable and could not be ignored. Faith knew she couldn't hide forever, because waiting too long would mean that the challenge would undermine her enjoyment and progress. So, with determination and a number of sacrifices, she decided to spring into action and pick things up again when the time was right.

But what happened to the others in the enclave in the meantime? Lacking the insights Faith gave them, they were soon at the mercy of the unpredictability of the wolves that crossed their path. Without Faith's guidance, some were overwhelmed by this danger. Others, however, tried to continue their intuitive approach, albeit with less success. The enclave, once brimming with intuitive energy, now felt the shadow of uncertainty and loss. The bounty was just as far away.

Gains and Troubles Lifferalitoye had already foreseen the possibility of wolves and other strange threats in the valley, taking them into account as well as possible, and were therefore better prepared for what was to come. They knew that it would be a major challenge and that a concerted effort would be needed to overcome this task. Gains had long ago realized that every problem brings its intrinsic opportunities. His belief was that even in the most unexpected situations, such as the presence of wolves, there was potential for growth and improvement. But he also understood that this potential could only be exploited by working together and addressing this opportunity with the right strategy.

Troubles, as a sceptic of the team, was thorough in her approach. She recognized the serious threat posed by the wolves and worked to find effective and proactive solutions to safeguard the village and its inhabitants. Her thorough analysis of possible pitfalls and dangers ensured that the village did not take unnecessary risks. She worked closely with Gains to ensure that his ideas were implemented in a safe and actionable manner.

In the village of Gains and Troubles, various measures were taken to keep the wolves at bay. Gains, with his innovative spirit, had set up some 'decoy targets' on the outskirts of the village. These were designed to attract the attention of the wolves and lead them away from the village and its immediate surroundings. It was a clever diversion that led the wolves astray and gave the residents valuable time to further prepare and respond to this unexpected threat. Fire pits and torches were quickly placed in strategic positions around the village. These not only provided light and warmth, but also functioned as a deterrent to the wolves, who are usually wary of fire. In case of direct confrontations, residents could also quickly light extra fires if necessary to keep the wolves at a safe distance.

Gains also designed special wolf traps that were placed at carefully chosen points around the village. These traps were designed to efficiently and effectively hold the wolves without seriously injuring them. Gains also proposed creating a demarcated and controlled wolf area outside the village. This could later also serve as a kind of tourist attraction where visitors could safely watch the wolves from a distance. In this way, the village could generate extra income through tourism.

With her thorough analysis, Troubles named specific areas where pitfalls for wolves could be dug. These pits were covered with light and soft materials so that wolves would fall into them without suffering significant injury. Gains also came up with the opportunity to set up a wolf education centre. This centre would provide information about wolves, their behaviour and the role they play in the ecosystem. It would provide an educational experience for locals and visitors alike.

Through these measures, Gains and Troubles managed to keep the wolves at bay and use them to their advantage. By proactively guaranteeing the safety of the village, they were able to rake in an extra bounty. Not much later, Serena Dipity joined them, looking for protection from the wolves. Through collaboration and proactive action, they created space for even more souls, and together they developed even more innovative solutions to strengthen the valley and to address and seize both the challenges and opportunities that the wolves brought. Together, they were determined to protect the valley and turn this crisis into even more growth and development.

So, the story of the valley continued. The audience at the networking event was reminded by the valley, with all its adventures and challenges, of the valuable lessons that people can learn on their path in life. But the pack of wolves was only part of this fascinating and never-ending adventure. It is the choices one makes and the actions that follow that determine how one traverses the valley of life. The inhabitants of the valley learned that through cooperation, being prepared for difficulties, and seizing opportunities, they could not only survive, but also grow and prosper, no matter what challenges came their way.

With determination and cooperation, the inhabitants of the valley managed to control the threat of the wolves and turn the tide. The valley recovered and returned to its prosperous state, in which everyone could once again enjoy gaining a new bounty. But as in any growing and thriving environment, challenges present themselves again and again.

Serena, the cheerful traveller, now had to be more in line with the story that Troubles and Gains wrote. She learned that forward thinking, flexibility, and collaboration were crucial to success, even in the most unexpected situations. Faith slowly but steadily resumed her progress in the valley, seizing opportunities she had previously missed, and soon her intuitive approach brought her back to the forefront of entrepreneurship.

Dodger had somewhat lost faith in his boss and worked intensively to restore his relationship with the villagers. He realized that trust was the basis for cooperation and achieving results. Despite his good advice and efforts, Dodger was also faced with the task of regaining the trust of his boss, Mr. Endever, given the far-reaching consequences of his decisions and the subsequent lack of confidence of all villagers.

In the end, Mr. Endever was replaced by Mrs. Gejarcee and her assistant, Mr. Tidau. Due to the events in the valley, there were ever more rules and guidelines, which created the need to also focus on compliance with legislative documents. Dodger understood the importance of gaining the trust of this new leadership team, as their support was crucial to implementing measures against the threat of wolves and other hidden dangers. He continued to advocate for collective efforts and stability under the new leadership, with the aim of restoring trust and working towards a safer future for the village.

After some time, the valley flourished like never before and everyone was able to collect the 'bounty' again.

"Plenty of bounty paves the way for a joyful life."

A Smart Move

Gains and Troubles analysed what had happened when the wolves appeared in the valley. This allowed them to continue their efforts with more precision and better protect the village and address weaknesses. They found that their strategies, while effective, could be vastly improved by circulating the best available information, with more clearly agreed forms of communication. The involvement and input of all villagers was also an essential element in this.

It happened one evening, when the sun with its golden glow was setting behind the hills. Gains and Troubles gathered the villagers around the central fire pit to discuss the latest wolf sightings and the effectiveness of traps and decoy targets. It was during this meeting that a young villager raised an important point.

"All these measures are great," she said, "but wouldn't it be even more effective if everyone knew exactly what was going on, what the goal was and if they were then able to decide for themselves what to do to achieve the common goal? Sometimes it feels like we're all working in different directions."

Gains and Troubles exchanged pensive glances. They knew she was right. The village relied on their individual innovations and strategies, but there was little coordination or sharing of critical information. It was time to change that.

Gains, with his innovative spirit, proposed to create a universally approved approach to communication. This approach would make it possible to collect and disseminate accurate and up-to-date information on the activity of wolves, the status of the traps and any new strategies that are being developed. It would also serve as a way for villagers to share new threats or opportunities with each other or pass on their own observations and suggestions. This would allow the best available information to be provided.

Troubles, with her analytical skills, also suggested a system to keep track of this information and update it regularly. "We need clear goals," she said, "and a way to measure our progress. We need to set up regular patrols and reporting schedules so that we always have the latest information."

Within weeks, the difference was clear. With everyone now on the same page, the village's efforts became more coordinated and were carried out with greater efficiency. They were able to respond more quickly to wolf sightings, adapt their strategies based on the latest data, and ensure that all measures contributed to the common goal of security and prosperity.

Gains and Troubles took turns leading the weekly meetings to further refine the information, share insights, and encourage open discussion. They also emphasized the importance of clear communication and aligning goals with the overall purpose of the village and valley.

One day, when they were looking at the latest reports, Gains had an additional idea. "Why don't we expand our efforts and create a training for everyone with training sessions on communication and decision-making? If everyone understands the importance of these skills, we will be even stronger." Because it was clear to decision-making that each villager needed to be able to make good use of the same dynamic, flexible, and iterative process that Troubles and Gains used to acquire their bounty. This structured and comprehensive approach would use the best available information to ensure timely and accurate decisions. This inclusive and tailor-made approach would definitely benefit the villagers, the village and even the whole valley, as it could also consider the human and cultural factors. Furthermore, it could also be used to improve what needed to be improved.

The comprehensive education plan quickly became a cornerstone of the village's success. Villagers learned not only about wolves, but also about effective communication, goal setting, setting criteria and teamwork to arrive at solutions. They practiced these skills and became more adept at making decisions that also benefited the entire community.

As time went on, the village where Gains and Troubles resided became known not only for its clever wolf deterrents, but also for its exemplary communication and decision-making practices. Visitors from other villages came to them to learn their methods as well. The village flourished both as a safe haven and a centre of knowledge and innovation.

Gains and Troubles had discovered a crucial truth: that the key to their success lay not only in their individual innovations, but also in their ability to collect and disseminate correct information, set clear goals, and ensure that everyone could make aligned decisions. By doing so, they had created a community that was resilient, informed, and united in its efforts to protect, grow, and thrive.

Thus, the village of Gains and Troubles continued to develop, as a testament to the power of information, communication, and cooperation.

Another Challenge for the Valley

In the valley, where sunshine and soft clouds reigned supreme for a long time, dark clouds suddenly broke loose. The idyllic period of carelessness and happiness was rudely interrupted. The inhabitants of the valley were increasingly confronted with unpleasant surprises. Lately, there has been increasingly fiercer headwind. And relentless rain showers dominated the atmosphere.

Serena was happy that the problem of the wolves was under control and after a while had picked up her old habit of going through life free and happy. Serena Dipity had always lived in the moment. She enjoyed the sun on her face, the soft grass under her feet, and the bountiful bounty the valley had to offer her. Preparation was unnecessary for her. Why worry when everything is going well? While others were planning or worried about the future, Serena still believed that life would always be kind to her.

But beautiful songs don't last long. The dark clouds that gathered over the valley seemed harmless at first. Serena kept her gaze on the sun even as the first raindrops fell. "It will blow over again," she thought, and she continued her carefree path. But when the rain turned into a torrent and the water began to rise, even Serena's optimism could no longer protect her. The paths she had always relied on became treacherously slippery. The sucking mud stopped her, and the rising water washed away her bounty.

Serena realized too late that her lack of preparation had put her in a precarious position. She had become trapped in a flooded area, far away from her familiar routes. For the first time, she

"Clinging to old paradigms and beliefs won't yield new bounties."

felt the fear that everything she valued could be lost forever. Her relaxed attitude, which had always served her, now turned out to be her greatest weakness. It was time to act – but Serena didn't know where to start.

Dodger had known for some time that harsh weather could pose a threat to his village. He had therefore devised a plan to drain excess water to a collection system that would protect the entire neighbourhood. But that plan never got off the ground. It was seen as too expensive. "No costs without benefits," he heard repeatedly. But when the rain continued and the river burst its banks, the village was in danger. Yet he also got the lid on the nose now. "Why should we pay for a problem that mainly affects the low areas?" some leaders of the higher areas had said, because many clung to their own interests, so that the proposed investment was mainly seen as a cost and therefore not incurred.

When the rain continued, what Dodger had feared finally happened. The river burst its banks, and the water began to flow through the streets. Sandbag barriers were quickly erected everywhere, but this only happened around their own homes or rather neighbourhoods. While certain areas were completely flooded, others remained just dry. The residents began to distrust each other, and cooperation seemed further away than ever.

Dodger did his best to control the situation and limit the damage. But his focus was now mainly on saving his own neighbourhood. He knew that the solution lay in cooperation but felt trapped in the limitations that others imposed on him. Like her predecessor, Mrs. Gejarcee opted for a pragmatic approach with a short-term view. "We protect who brings the most value. The rest must fend for themselves," she said very decisively.

A considerable number of residents lost their bounty completely. Others barely held out, but everyone felt the consequences. The limited supplies and the lack of coordination meant that the bounty was seriously affected. While everyone was focused on their own interests, the village, as a whole, missed the opportunity to become stronger together.

Faith Destiny at once sensed that the bad weather was more than a temporary inconvenience. The successive showers threatened to change her world. She had always been confident in her ability to see opportunities, find solutions, and make her part of the valley thrive. But this time it was different. The water rose, the paths became slippery and impassable, and her intuition, normally a source of strength, seemed to let her down. For the first time in years, Faith felt lost.

Faith's attempts to keep her part of the valley dry failed miserably. She felt how the bounty almost literally slipped away. "How could I be so blind?" she asked herself. She had always trusted her instincts, but now she realized that certain challenges require more than intuition. She had no systems or structures that could support her intuition. As the chaos mounted, Faith found herself relying too much on her own ability to make decisions. With no help from others, no plan to pass on, she became overwhelmed.

While others focused on individual solutions or intuitive responses, Troubles and Gains believed in a comprehensive and integrated approach. For them, it was all about collaboration, future-oriented vision and the power of collective intelligence.

Long before the rain clouds gathered, they wondered, "What if?" This simple question led to extensive discussions with the other inhabitants of their valley. They started with analyses of the various sources of risk that not only identified potential threats but also uncovered hidden opportunities.

Troubles, with her keen insight into weak spots and potential problems, foresaw how heavy rainfall could hit the valley and their bounty. She worked methodically on plans to minimize the impact of the excessive rainfall. Gains, on the other hand, brought energy and creativity to the process. He saw opportunities to use the abundant water as a source of growth and prosperity.

Jointly, they convinced their community to act together. By creating strategic flood plains and retention basins, they not only protected the land from flooding, but also ensured a more sustainable water supply. These systems also gave them the prospect of growing new crops, which previously seemed impossible. Gains even saw the opportunity to build hydroelectric power plants, which would allow their valley to generate more energy and trade more easily with other valleys.

But their strength was not only in coming up with technical solutions. They understood that real progress comes from working together. Gains involved the other residents in the design process and took their ideas seriously. Troubles organized sessions where everyone could share their concerns, ensuring that every perspective was thoroughly considered. In this way, they created a culture of trust, in which everyone knew that their voice was important, and the best information could be put to effective use.

Their approach went beyond just technical measures. They taught the community how to deal with uncertainty in a more flexible way. They invested in training so that everyone understood how decisions were made and how they could contribute to them themselves. Thanks to their efforts, their

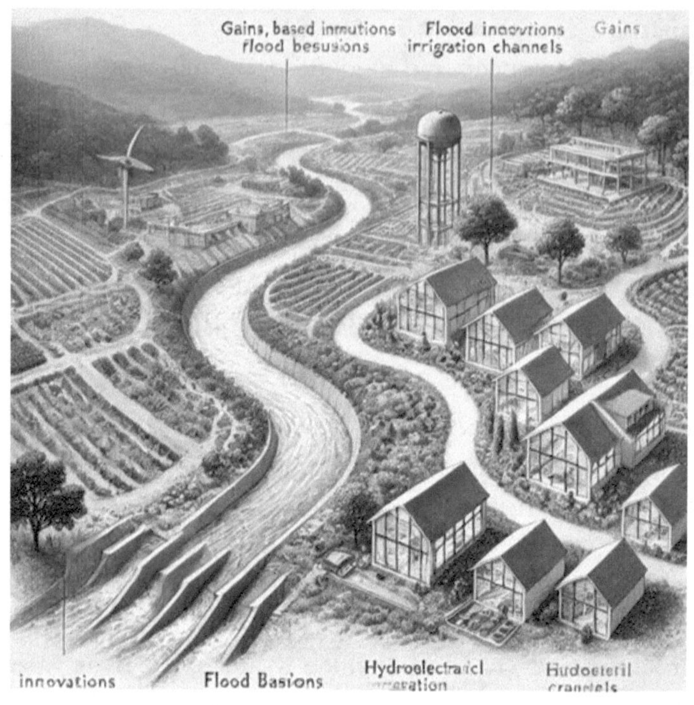

"Effectively managing risks builds confidence."

"Staying focused on the bounty makes it easier to achieve."

community grew into a learning community that was prepared for whatever the future would bring.

Gains and Troubles recorded their experiences in a number of statements for their community. They called it their "manifesto". It was a document that could be an inspiration for every inhabitant of the valley.

The "manifesto" sounds like this:

1. Risk management Creates value and Protects value.

The valley flourishes when you are focused on progress. Plant crops, build new paths, and make sure what you create is sturdy enough to withstand storms. Protecting value starts with creating value.

2. Integrate risk management.

Value is created when risk management is intertwined with everything you do. Build not only a shelter from wolves, but also roads that allow trade and cooperation. Growth and value are in the whole.

3. Be structured and comprehensive.

Creating value means taking the entire valley into account. Don't just protect what you have but make plans that include everything and everyone — from your crops to the river you drink from.

4. Adapt risk management to the situation.

Value comes when you create solutions that fit the challenges. Build strong homes against the storm, dig irrigation canals where drought prevails, and create a valley that thrives despite the many dangers and challenges.

5. Make it inclusive.

The valley flourishes if everyone can contribute. Whether you're chasing away wolves or planting fields, every talent and effort can help create and protect value.

6. Make sure it's dynamic.

Value grows by moving with change. A storm can cause damage but also create new opportunities for better construction techniques. Be flexible and keep building your future.

7. Rely on the best available information.

Value comes from wisdom. Pay attention to the signs: tracks in the ground, the position of the sun and the advice of the elderly in the valley. Valuable information helps you turn problems into opportunities.

8. Consider human and cultural factors.

Creating value means understanding what drives people. A proud hunter, a patient farmer and a creative builder each bring unique contributions. Culture and cooperation allow the valley to flourish sustainably.

9. Strive for continuous improvement.

Every challenge brings an opportunity to become stronger. Use lessons from the storms and wolves to make the valley even more fertile. Growth is a continuous process of learning and adapting.

Epilogue

Iris Tetynohko finished her story and addressed the gathering of experts around her, her voice sounding steady and thoughtful. "Dear friends, I hope that the story of this valley and its inhabitants can connect with your experiences in business and that it teaches us that there are different ways to deal with the fundamental truth of a world full of uncertainties. Carefree is good for a while but is not a solution for unexpected things that can be threatening and is therefore no guarantee of a successful future. It is also true that a lack of structure and excessive reliance on the individual for decisions can hinder proper planning and growth. But it is also true that a lack of agreement, with a focus on the short term without a serious long-term vision, does not lead to sustainable results either."

The attendees nodded in agreement. After all, they had met many storms and wolves in their careers and had sometimes paid a price for them.

Iris continued her argument and said thoughtfully: "I myself have learned a lot through trial and error. And much of what I have experienced myself I recognised in this story of the valley and its inhabitants. Faith Destiny reminded me of the power of intuition, but I also learned that structure and planning are indispensable in turbulent times. Serena Dipity showed me that carefree gives more flexibility, but without preparation it offers no resilience. Dodger Dagner showed me that caution can save lives, but that cooperation and initiative are crucial to achieving what is needed. Each of them reacted differently to the events, but they were less prepared than Troubles and Gains, which showed that a shared vision, teamwork and a long-term focus not only protect your organization and society but also allow it to flourish."

She continued: "The lesson here is clear: while caution and stability are essential, they must be balanced with flexibility, creativity and the presence of shared objectives. Effective communication and inclusive decision-making are the cornerstones of a resilient and prosperous community. We must learn to embrace change, harness our collective intelligence, and make aligned decisions that support us all. In this way, we can create a society that not only weathers crises but also grows and flourishes sustainably. Let's take these lessons to heart and build a future where we are prepared, united, and always ready to turn challenges into opportunities."

The crowd of experts listened silently to Iris's words. Her story also reflected their ambitions, their fears and the essence of their entrepreneurship. It was a catalyst for deep reflection on their own individual situations and the choices they would make in pursuit of their own bounty.

The networking event took on a new dimension that evening. It was not only a platform to connect and share successes, but also a place where dreams, resilience and the art of dealing with life's uncertainties came together.

And so began their journey into a new world, where the labyrinth of challenges and possibilities would challenge their perceptions of success, risk, and the pursuit of what really matters.

Geraint Kammens saw that the group was left with a deep sense of contemplation and a shared curiosity about how their own stories might unfold in the face of both opportunities and setbacks.

Geraint therefore wondered who he could identify with the most. What kind of risk management could be found in his organization? Just on good luck? Managing risk according to gut feeling? Structured with a focus on the negative, focused on inventory, advice and reporting? Or integrated into a corporate culture focused on objectives and continuous improvement? He knew what he would prefer ... You too?

Appendix

The distinct parts of the metaphor

1.   The valley:

The valley stands for our society teeming with opportunities, but it also hides many dangers and threats. It's what life is all about. When we pursue a goal, there will always be possibilities, but the choices we make will have both positive and negative aspects. Choices determine repeatedly which positive aspects can be played out and which negative aspects are offered a chance to realize themselves.

2.   The bounty:

The bounty is what one ultimately gets in life by making efforts. It is the fruit of one's work and the objective one pursues. There are always different options to obtain those fruits. Making the right choices has not become easier today. In a general sense, it comes down to obtaining the right information in advance so that you can choose the best path to your "bounty". Which resources can help you with this and what things stand in the way? It is the positive sources of risk that can help you move forward that also decide which negative aspects of risk can become reality. Finding the right balance and managing both types of risk sources is what ultimately leads to sustainable success.

As you travel through the valley, it quickly becomes clear that each resident has a unique approach to navigating this enchanting, yet treacherous landscape. Each character symbolizes a type of business, with her own strengths, weaknesses, and ways of dealing with uncertainty and bounty. These contrasts made the differences between the companies particularly visible.

3.   Serena Dipity: The spontaneous small self-employed

Serena Dipity

Serena embodied the independent entrepreneur who works without much preparation or structure. Her "Carpe diem" motto reflects a complete confidence in the moment. Serena lives without worries for tomorrow, reaping the benefits of her journey without much thought about the consequences or preparing for challenges. This approach works as long as conditions stay favourable, but the pitfalls become visible with the first storm. Serena has no buffer or plan to keep her upright when the trails get slippery, and the mud locks her down. Her story shows the fragility of an approach without foresight and without preparation: the loss of opportunities in tough times.

4.   Faith Destiny: The intuitive SME

Faith Destiny

Faith Destiny is the embodiment of the successful, yet intuitively driven SME owner. Her exceptional instincts often help her to see opportunities in the valley and seize her bounty quickly and efficiently. She fully trusts her personal abilities, which makes her venture successful in predictable situations. However, her reliance on intuition and lack of structured support makes her vulnerable to unexpected storms. When circumstances become chaotic and complexity increases, she may become overwhelmed. Faith's story highlights the limitations of an approach that relies heavily on a single leader and their personal skills without the backup of robust systems or teams to support the organization.

5. **Dodger Dagner, Mr. Endever, Ms. Gejarcee, and Mr. Tidau: The Structured, But Siloed (Silo) Organization**

Dodger Dagner

Dodger Dagner represents the risk manager of an organization that is heavily focused on structure and formal risk management, but where silos and poor collaboration are often an obstacle. His meticulous approach, aimed at avoiding dangers, provides a certain stability, but more than once clashes with the adventurous and short-term oriented style of managers such as Mr. Endever. Their conflicting priorities often result in tensions and missed opportunities. When the organization comes under new leadership, the focus often shifts to compliance with new rules and legislation, which further widens the gap between risk managers and executives. This type of organization illustrates how a lack of alignment and collaboration can lead to inefficiency and loss of bounty, even with a robust risk management system in place.

6. Gains and Troubles Lifferalitoye: The Integrated Learning Organization

Gains and Troubles Lifferalitoye

The collaboration between Gains and Troubles symbolizes a mature organization where leadership and risk management go hand in hand. Gains is the visionary leader who sees opportunities and explores new possibilities, while Troubles proposes the manager who provides these ambitions with practical strategies and thorough risk analyses. Together, they worked not only to overcome challenges, but to transform uncertainty into growth. By collaborating with all relevant stakeholders, both inside and outside the valley, they create innovative solutions, such as "hydroelectric power plants" and "irrigation systems", which both mitigate negative risks and added more value. This organization, a model of integrated risk management and collective intelligence, shows that success depends not only on plans and structures, but also on collaboration and continuous improvement.

Comparing these four figures gives a clear picture of the different approaches to enterprises:

- The small self-employed person without structure: Spontaneous and flexible, but vulnerable to change.
- The intuitive SME: Fast and decisive, but dependent on the capabilities of one leader.
- The structured, siloed organization: Risk-averse and focused on compliance, but often inefficient due to internal contradictions.
- The integrated learning organization: Innovative, resilient and successful through cooperation and balance between vision and practical implementation.

Each approach offers lessons, but only the last demonstrates a sustainable and future-proof strategy in the complex valley of uncertainty and bounty.

7. Concepts, properties and anagrams

- *Anagrams & concepts:*

Geraint Kammens	Risk Management
Mr. Esoco	COSO ERM
Sandra Dolts	Old Standards
Iris Tetynohko	ISOThirtyOneK (ISO 31000)
Lifferalitoye	Reality of life
Gejarcee	GRC Governance, Risk & Compliance
Tidau	Audit

- *Properties*

Serena Dipity:	Serendipity = A predisposition to make desired discoveries by chance.
Faith Destiny:	Complete faith, or trust in something or someone and in a future that someone or something will have.
Dodger Dagner:	Dodging Danger = Avoiding negative risk
Gains:	Profit (Positive risk)
Troubles:	Hardship (Negative risk)

Intentionally Left Blank

Intentionally Left Blank

www.ingramcontent.com/pod-product-compliance
Lightning Source LLC
LaVergne TN
LVHW091621170726

843492LV00007B/2536